First published in the United Kingdom by
Life Foundation Publications,
Nant Ffrancon, Bethesda, Bangor, North Wales LL57 3LX
E-mail: enquiries@lifefoundation.org.uk
www.lifefoundation.org.uk

ISBN 1 873606 18 4

Printed by Biddles Limited, Woodbridge Park Estate,
Woodbridge Road, Guildford, Surrey, GU1 1DA.

Printed on 80gsm High White Antique Wove

Life Foundation Publications

Plant A Tree

For every title published we plant and care for a tree

The Life Foundation is a team of committed individuals from a wide
range of backgrounds, working together and dedicated to developing
the highest potential in people. We teach powerful self-development
techniques that integrate body, heart and mind, promote physical
well-being, emotional balance, successful relationships and personal
fulfilment. Our aim is to transform the world by giving people the
tools to transform themselves.

Awakening Soulforce

Dr Mansukh Patel

Compiled and edited by Yamuna devi

LIFE FOUNDATION PUBLICATIONS, NORTH WALES, UK

Dedication

To people all over the world
who are seeking freedom

Contents

Foreword   8

Introduction   10

Part One

A Living Talisman   13

Part Two

Ignition Point - over to you   31

Question Yourself   32

The Power of Intention   34

Soulforce Talismans   35

The Practical Application   36

Hold on to your Talisman   37

Part Three

Soulforce Talismans   39

Part Four

The Golden Eagle Sequence   65

Reflection   74

About the Author   78

Foreword

It is now nearly four years since I and my partner Jon James were taken hostage in Chechnya. Our capture marked the beginning of fourteen and a half months of the most testing time we have ever endured. Fortunately our interest in a holistic approach to living had given us many tools that helped us to survive captivity. We were held in small, windowless, airless rooms under immense psychological pressure, subject to physical and mental torture. Through yoga, meditation and visualisation, Tai Chi and Chi Kung combined with our belief in the power of prayer, we were able to survive with our health and sanity intact.

When we were eventually freed we heard how Mansukh Patel had inspired thousands of people to conduct a prayer vigil on our behalf. This made a deep impression on both myself and Jon and we were even more impressed when we eventually met him and some of his Life Foundation colleagues. We found that many of the exercises they were teaching in Dru Yoga were very similar to those we had been using in captivity.

I have had the privilege of being able to observe Mansukh teaching de-traumatisation techniques first-hand. I have to say it is the most inspirational teaching I have ever seen. He has a profound understanding of how to transform trauma in the body and mind and to recreate inspiration and hope in people who have been psychologically damaged by the experiences of war.

The gems of wisdom and understanding that come through this book epitomise the quality of his understanding. I have seen the Golden Eagle Sequence in action and I know it works. I truly believe that the wisdom and information contained in these pages offer a definitive way to bring about freedom - for the individual as well as a whole country. Just by beginning this process we start to change our lives. This understanding is here for all of us to read, absorb and work with in this little book so that we too can reach beyond what we perceive to be our human limitations by starting to use our spiritual power, our *soulforce*. Eventually all we do will be enthused by the power of divine love - the key to our freedom. As Goethe once said, *'Whatever you can do, or dream you can do, begin it. Boldness has genius, power and magic in it.'*

Camilla Carr

Introduction

This book is an invitation to express yourself and your life in a totally new way - one that uses soul power. It has been born out of a real life situation - one that we normally only read about in the newspapers. May it stir your heart and excite the part of you that is longing for freedom.

The pulse that surges through this book is the reawakening of hope and faith inspired by the plight of people who are living in a war zone. It is their deepest yearning and pain that has brought it into being. The substance of *Awakening Soulforce* has arisen from the personal experiences of forty-five aid workers - people who have dedicated their lives to helping their countrymen resurrect some kind of hope and stability amidst the turmoil of invasion and the devastation of war.

In their presence I felt the urgency of their situation in a way that tore at my heart. Over a period of only three and a half days I came to understand how a nation can feel completely lost and forgotten by the world. What is even more poignant is that their experience highlights the dilemma of every human being. I realised that everyone has the potential to effect such a change, because I witnessed these individuals igniting the technique I have outlined here to the highest degree. The impact it had upon me personally was such that I have written this book, just days after the event, in order to share this revelation with the world.

My deepest wish is for you, the reader, to be able to awaken to as much joy and excitement as I have felt in writing it. Once we make a conscious choice to read, memorise and then act upon knowledge, it cannot fail to change us and the way we express our lives. Awakening and expressing soul power is what I call a freedom-based activity. Something emerges from the very centre of our being that is so empowering it heals not only ourselves, but everyone around us.

My message is that *you have the same power* - to create a bridge between two worlds - the worlds of despair and hope, hatred and love, war and peace. I invite you to take up the challenge and transform your own life in the process.

Mansukh Patel

'When you are inspired by some great purpose,
some extraordinary project,
all your thoughts break their bonds.
Your mind transcends limitations,
your mind expands in every direction
and you find yourself in a new,
great and wonderful world.' - Patanjali

Part One

A Living Talisman

A living Talisman

Mahatma Gandhi, who has always been my greatest hero and role model, had a Talisman which guided his life. It was simply this. Whenever he was about to do something he would first think of the poorest person he had ever seen, imagine their face and then ask himself if what he was about to do would benefit that person. If not, he simply would not act. The effect of this resolve was that everything he did was fired and motivated by his great desire to benefit others' lives through his actions.

It was a great and noble way to live and the result of living by this principle was that he was able to free over 350 million people from 300 years of foreign rule. Traditionally a Talisman is said to be a stone that is imbued with a magical power, but as Gandhi demonstrated, it can be a resolution or unshakeable conviction that carries power.

Soulforce

Gandhi was probably the most important man of the twentieth century because he demonstrated over and over again throughout his life that peace can be very practical. He always maintained that the secret of his indestructible satyagraha movement lay in the power of their *soulforce*. He said that this force is lying dormant within each and every living being. My life has been dedicated to helping people to understand and discover this power - to rise above self-imposed limitations and reach their own greatness. Wherever I am, whatever I am doing, I am always thinking about different ways to encourage people to achieve this.

Finding fulfilment

We are continually confronted by a suffering humanity which is desperately seeking solutions. I especially feel the plight of our younger generation that is deeply seeking a way to find real and lasting fulfilment. By the grace of Gandhi's example and through the efforts of my parents, I have been endowed with the scientific and spiritual knowledge that can really help others and for this I am eternally grateful. It brings purpose and meaning to my own life. I believe, as Gandhi did, that it is only when this *soulforce* is awakened within us that we can find the ultimate sense of fulfilment we all seek. Whether you are dealing with personal trauma in your family or the mass murder of war, ultimately this knowledge of soulforce is the greatest gift that has been given to us in the last hundred years. Now we need to take it into the third millennium and *live* it.

We have seen how Gandhi made soulforce work and how he applied it, but we must not allow ourselves to think that it was just something that he alone worked with and believed in. In freeing India he demonstrated to us *all* that freedom can be achieved at all levels, through the awakening of this individual soulforce factor. Of course the method of this awakening is different in every set of circumstances.

Teaching de-traumatisation

Together with three of my colleagues Andrew Wells, Savitri MacCuish and Peter Legge, I was recently called out to teach de-traumatisation techniques to a group of forty-five child psychologists and counsellors who were working inside a war zone. As with much of our work I cannot say where it was. In such sensitive areas it is vital to maintain our neutrality so that we can help all sides in their efforts to regain peace. We were staying in an old sanatorium which had been built on the edge of the ocean, some distance from the scene of conflict. This gave all the participants a welcome break from their homeland's constant reminders of war, especially for those who were living close to the violence. Our group members were all working with badly traumatised children, desperately seeking to help them to heal the emotional scars of war. Even now, as often as two or three times a week as they travel in to work with the children, they have to stop and dive to the ground because of the sudden eruption of a shoot-out.

At any moment, they can be stopped and questioned by the military and if they are young men there is a thirty percent chance they will be taken away and beaten - or worse.

Living on the edge

These were rugged people who were living on the edge, but with a tremendous sense of dignity. They were desperately trying to deal with their own personal trauma as well as that of the children and their countrymen. I was impressed by how well they had managed to keep their spirits up and maintain their sanity under circumstances that would have destroyed most ordinary people. At the same time I could feel a subtle tension hiding behind their laughter and playfulness. The experience of years of war had definitely taken its toll and deep down they were all feeling the tremendous weight of their plight - and a sense of hopelessness about their future as a nation. We had worked with them on many occasions and knew how much our techniques and methods had helped them to cope with their own traumas. This time, however, I felt we needed to introduce a deeper element to help them to rekindle their hope and enthusiasm in the face of their waning strength.

What could I do?

I only had a few days and the hours were slipping by rapidly. As I sat by the edge of the sea contemplating the whole situation I thought about Gandhi and asked myself what he would have done. These people needed to be able to tap into another level of energy altogether - a power that allows ordinary people to endure and overcome the most impossible circumstances. How was I to awaken this kind of power into their lives in such a short time? What was it that I as an individual could give them that went beyond all the techniques I had learned from my twenty-five years as a peacemaker?

And then I remembered how Gandhi had always said that the power of one person's soulforce is enough to change the world. Tapping into this force enabled Nelson Mandela not only to survive twenty-six years of incarceration, but to emerge smiling and triumphant, ready to take on the presidency of his country. I realised then that nothing less than the power of soulforce was going to work for these psychologists and counsellors. This was the only thing that would enable them to go forward with renewed enthusiasm to face the next phase of their lives.

How to do it?

Of course Gandhi had his own methods and approaches that created social movements and models to implement soulforce in society. His power came from his spiritual practice of silence, meditation and reading the Bhagavad Gita. My parents, who were Gandhians all their lives, were also custodians of their own indigenous tradition - that of Dru Yoga. Having had this knowledge imparted to me, I now had to draw upon the wisdom of that tradition to create a model that would work for these people.

As I stood in front of these forty-five people, I began

by impressing upon them the importance of knowing that they were not a forgotten people without a future. I assured them that many people cared about them and were willing to help. I asked my translator to make sure they understood that there were thousands of people all over the world who believed in them and supported their cause. She started to cry at this point, momentarily unable to continue. Here was a very successful woman whose experiences of the war and the horrors she had witnessed had changed her dramatically. She now lives a life that is completely dedicated to helping others. Another woman started to cry and then one young man, leaning forward with elbows on his knees, bowed his head and started to sob quietly. A tremendous wave of feeling engulfed the room as the depth of their emotion affected everyone and I realised then that they did indeed feel that they were a lost culture, abandoned by the world. It was so gratifying to know that I had something to offer them that could help to heal this immense sense of loss and deep loneliness.

Invoking the power of a personal intention

I was also aware that because of their intense

suffering there was a part of them that felt the world owed them something. There was a feeling of expectancy, which was creating a slightly passive attitude. To fully participate in a solution involving their soulforce, however, they needed to be very alert and awake at every level.

So I began by telling them about a technique that could awaken a power within them that would help to resolve both personal and political crises. I explained that if they could persuade 0.1% of their population to do this technique with the *intention* of helping their country, within a few months they would start to move towards real and lasting peace.

I reminded them that because Gandhi's *intention* was to free India, by believing this he conclusively proved that soulforce can be evoked and utilised effectively in every possible circumstance - even when up against an apparently unchallengeable military force. That same possibility had now arrived at their doorstep. Already everyone present had become more alert and was listening very carefully.

'But I am not sure if I can teach it to you....' I added.

As I said this, the atmosphere dramatically changed and a tense silence enveloped the room. I went on to explain that if they were not ready for it and not really serious about achieving freedom in their lives, it simply would not work for them. They needed to have an aspiration and vision equal in magnitude to that of such great men as Martin Luther King and Mahatma Gandhi. The atmosphere intensified even more.

'But if any of you feel that you are a person who has the yearning to use this approach, someone who really wants to achieve the same potential as someone like Gandhi...,' I said, deliberately challenging them. I wanted to see just how willing they were to engage in something greater than life itself. Everyone's eyes began to widen and it felt as if the whole roomful of people was holding its breath.

'...meet me later this evening by the forest grove down by the sea.' And I left it up to them to decide to take it further.

Turning point - from doubt to faith

One woman asked to see me privately. She challenged me quite fiercely about the fact that I could be raising false hopes in these broken people. Of course she was talking about herself, for there was an anguished look in her eyes. She was desperately soul-searching, at the same time afraid to believe this was going to work. How would she cope with yet another bitter disappointment? I explained to her that what I was offering was not hypothetical. Utilising the power of soulforce is a practical solution that has already been seen to work for people like Gandhi, Martin Luther King and Nelson Mandela as well as many other unsung heroes. And, I added gently, apart from all this, having already lost everything, what else could she lose by trying something that might just resurrect her hope?

Something in her eyes began to soften. She was looking at me in a different way and began to thank me for taking the time to offer a helping hand for no personal reward. It takes time for people to understand that there could be people who find joy in offering their lives to help others. But what a privilege it is to share a universal approach to awakening this soulforce power which embraces all, reaching beyond the boundaries of any dogma or creed.

The power of a living commitment

I was very happy to see over two thirds of the group gather on the shores of the sea, their eyes blazing with determination. I knew then that these people were definitely going to take the information and use it in a way that would make a huge difference to their lives. But what was to actually materialise during this event was to take even me by surprise.

Please imagine the scene. Thirty people silhouetted against the setting sun in front of the sea performing the awesomely powerful Golden Eagle Sequence *with the intention of bringing peace to their war-torn land.* Suddenly they were standing tall, firm and solid, their faces open and determined. They looked like warriors as they stood boldly offering their dynamism, creativity and power. Is it really possible to change the destiny of a nation in a moment? I believe so - because I observed the extraordinary power they generated together.

These people were standing in front of me with all their emotional, physical and mental energy available to them. Everything they had experienced in the past had brought them to a point of pure focus where they knew they were standing on the interface between all that had gone before and everything that was to come. I knew that they were creating their own future - I could *feel* it. I was reminded of the words of the French poet, Guillaume Appollinaire:

Come to the edge, he said.
No, we are afraid.
Come to the edge, he said.
They came, he pushed them... and they flew.

A personal revelation

I have taught the Golden Eagle Sequence all over the world in many different circumstances, and I have always known it to be a tool which has immense power. But the people in front of me were bringing the technique alive in a way that I had never before experienced. What was the difference? I think it was that they were all one hundred percent present, giving themselves to the process at every level - physically, mentally and emotionally with *full faith*. Suddenly I was seeing it as a living formula actually taking *root* in the lives of these people who were becoming living generators and conductors of the power of *soulforce*. I was amazed by the power that came from them. I have seen people's lives changed before, but in all my years of experience, I have never before witnessed such an immediate transformation. It could only have been because of the power of their *intention* and their intense faith and trust that they could *change the future of their country*.

The fire of hope

As the sun finally sank from view, the sky was streaked with glorious hues, which were reflected in the waters of the sea. As we all sat together on the grass the atmosphere was electric. People's eyes were shining and alive, excited by the possibilities they had glimpsed and enthused by the fire of hope that had once again been ignited within them.

Everyone, in their own way, expressed their experiences of the power they had felt. One young man said he felt so alive, as though his body was changing. An older woman said she felt her mind more composed, balanced and at peace. Another mentioned how he felt invigorated by a renewed positivity and enthusiasm. The head psychologist in charge of the children had become silent. There were tears in her eyes and as I looked at her a distinct change came over her face.

'We are going to do it,' she said with so much determination and conviction that it raised the hair on the back of my neck. In that moment I knew that right in front of my eyes they had become peacemakers, fired not by excitement, but by the very challenge of peacemaking.

The power of hope to motivate

But what were they going to do now that they had experienced this power and strength and its potential for self-transformation? I put this question to them. Momentarily there was complete silence and then one man suddenly jumped up, waving his arms expressively in the air and speaking very quickly in his own language. He said he had realised that this technique is universal and that it doesn't conflict with any faith, religion or tradition - it embraces everything. Everyone was nodding in agreement as he spoke. 'Now I understand how this can create freedom at so many different levels!' he said. 'Wouldn't it be amazing if we could teach this to *everyone* in our country and ask them to do the sequence at the same time every day with the same intention...?' He was so excited by this thought. 'I would like to go back and contact everyone we are working with in the refugee camps and different aid organisations - this involves dozens of camps. We will convince them that we have found a method that can really bring freedom to ourselves, our children and our country.'

The Pathans

I was immediately reminded of the story of Gandhi's historic meeting with the fierce Pathans who lived among the rugged mountains of the Khyber Pass in northern India. They were well known for their courage and fearlessness and passionate love for freedom as well as being greatly feared for their ruthless violence. Against the advice of all those around him, Gandhi had gone to meet them in the hills where they lived. He fearlessly approached them without any weapon and on seeing their guns asked them if they were afraid. They looked at him in amazement. These people were known for their extraordinary fearlessness.

'I have taught myself not to be afraid of anyone,' Gandhi explained, 'which is why I am unarmed. This is what non-violence means.' Their leader, Abdul Ghaffar Khan, was so affected by these words that he and his whole army of nearly 100,000 men decided to throw away their guns and join him. They became the first non-violent army and the backbone of Gandhi's non-violent revolution. Khan himself became Gandhi's devoted friend who followed him wherever he went, never leaving his side.

New warriors of peace

These people had the same kind of fire in their eyes and the same determination to fight for what they believed in. This was a living situation. It was real and happening right in front of me. It was part of a living history. We were *making* it. I looked at the crowd of eager faces and asked them if they really thought their countrymen would engage in this soulforce method. They assured me they would and in that moment I realised that by restoring the faith of these people and that of those they would help, my own faith had also increased a thousand times.

A new beginning

The next morning we woke up before sunrise and repeated the whole process for the sake of their nation. Now, as I write, there are hundreds of people all over that country doing this sequence at the same time every day. What an incredible vision of hope this offers us. We all have the same ability to transform our lives and thereby influence the lives of those around us and rise to the zenith of our potential. *Soulforce awakening* depends upon our own personal *intention* to expand our vision and to start to live and breathe for the benefit of all. If we are to follow Gandhi's example and therefore our own destiny, we need to embark on the exhilarating path of *putting others first*. This is only possible once we understand deeply that we have not just come here for ourselves and our own personal satisfaction.

Jai Jagat!

Once we are truly living for the welfare of others we start to change the world picture. We become like small candles lighting up the night of selfishness that has engulfed our world and its people. In this way we, like Gandhi, can achieve great victories for the human spirit. The secret to Gandhi's greatness lay in the fact that his selfish desires had been consumed by the fire of determination to work for the welfare of the world. His personal motto was 'Jai Jagat!' which means 'Victory to the world!' There was no thought of any personal gain whatsoever. The secret of every truly successful life is to select a selfless goal and to do everything we can to move towards it. There is no greater epitaph than *He lived for others*. This is not a fantastic dream. It is a living reality.

Part Two

Ignition Point - over to you

Question yourself

How do we, who are not living in a war zone, create the same kind of awakening of faith and powerful intention in our own lives? How do we bring ourselves to such a fine point of focus that *all* our energy becomes available to us? It is possible that you may be facing trials on a day to day basis that are just as poignant to you as the plight of those whose lives are engulfed by war.

You may not, however, be experiencing the same sense of urgency to create a catalyst in your own life. Paerhaps your life is not actually under threat, but you may be struggling with similar issues.

It is also possible that you are perfectly happy and content with your life although seeking to know the highest. One thing is certain, however. The same potential for awakening the power of your own soulforce is available to you now, in this moment, regardless of your individual circumstances.

Please ask yourself some fundamental questions:

How much does my life mean to me?

Do I want to access my very highest potential?

How can I use my life in such a powerful and effective way that it creates the maximum impact on the people around me?

The power of intention

Let me make it very clear that the technique that we taught in this detraumatisation training, the Golden Eagle Sequence, is not enough *by itself*. The most important factors are *why* you are doing it, what your *intention* is and how much *faith* you have in the process. The reason it worked for these people is that they were wanting to affect a change for the sake of their nation. *They were not doing it just for themselves.* This is the key.

As you align the way you live and act to make a difference to the lives of others, something extraordinary happens to you as an individual.

Something is awakened within you that is not accessible by any other means. This is the *soulforce awakening*. In order to make it work for *you*, please be very clear as to what your own intention is.

Soulforce Talismans

If you are willing to perform the Golden Eagle Sequence every day at the same time with this powerful intention of creating a change in the world, I would like to suggest that you incorporate another element into the process. This will help invoke the necessary potency. I am offering you twenty-four powerful spiritual truths which I call my *Talismans*. Each Talisman carries a unique quality which, when you work with it in your life, will alter your whole experience of everyday situations.

I have travelled all over the world, meeting people from every level of society from orphaned refugees in Bosnia to some of the richest people in places like America, Canada and Australia. Wherever I have been, without exception, I have witnessed the power of these truths working in every possible situation. I have found them to be just as potent and effective regardless of status, culture or circumstance for they are indestructible principles, built on the foundations of eternity. The words of each Talisman need to be savoured slowly, with deliberation and care. Please understand, these are very powerful truths - *when you live them.*

The Practical Application

Stage One

Each day, preferably at the same time, sit down and take one Talisman. Contemplate on its meaning for a few minutes.

Stage Two

Start to perform the *Golden Eagle Sequence* with the intention of helping someone else. It could be your family, friends, community or the world as a whole. Imbibe the **key words** of the Talisman at every stage.

Stage Three

When you reach the 8th position with palms facing outwards to the world please affirm, '**Let there be peace on the earth.**' *This is the ignition point* - where you offer yourself as a conductor and transmitter for peace.

Stage Four

Memorise the key words and find a way to take them with you into your day, repeating them regularly to remind you of the Talisman. You could write them down on a card and keep it in your pocket. Try different things like saying them out loud or repeating them silently over and over again.

Hold onto your Talisman

In the face of pain or rejection, hold onto your Talisman. To hold a constructive and positive thought in your mind when everything around you is moving in the opposite direction requires great courage. It may seem odd or awkward at first or even impossible to believe, but it will facilitate a change not only within yourself, but also in the world around you.

I suggest that you work with a sequence of twenty-four days using one Talisman each day.

After twenty-four days start again with the first Talisman so that you are always working with a cycle of twenty-four.

This process requires sincerity, regularity, persistence and *faith*. But as Jesus once said, you only need faith the size of a mustard seed for it to work.

Sometimes we can miss some of the greatest truths just because they appear to be too simple. Words carry a tremendous power - to either create or destroy. The Bible tells us that *In the beginning was the word,* indicating the creative power of one single spoken syllable. In India we have the Great Word, *Om*, which is said to contain not only the power of creation, but the power to liberate a human being. Similarly the Christian word *Amen* is said to empower the greatness of the human soul. Whether we realise it or not, every word we choose to use is influencing the quality of our lives.

Conscious awareness of this power creates an even deeper effect upon the subconscious and collective consciousness. Each time we repeat, write or read words, we are subtly changed by them. Gandhi once spoke the immortal words, *'My life is my message,'* to a reporter as he was boarding a train. I would like to see these words written at the front of every book - the Bible or the Gita, or every text book in every school and college. Imagine the implications of every person believing that they have the same power and potential as someone like Gandhi.

Part Three

Soulforce Talismans

Day 1

Keep a constant *yearning* to be
awake and fulfilled.

yearning

Day 2

Live your life with power and *courage*
so that others are inspired to do the same.

Day 3

Always follow the bidding of *your heart*.

Keywords   my heart

Day 4

The most important place is *here*.
The most important time is *now*.
The most important person is
the one in *front* of you.

be here now

Day 5

If you are always giving, you need time to
restore and replenish your own body and soul.
Rest in nature - and *silence*.

Day 6

Do not stop striving until you have reached the very *highest goal* for your life.

reach high

Day 7

The great task is to *awaken* oneself first
and then to help others to awaken.

awaken

Day 8

A life that is expressing *service*
in every moment is profound indeed.
Breathe in life and breathe out service.

serve others

Day 9

Forgiveness dissolves all suffering.

Keywords   **forgive**

Day 10

As you *share your light* with others your own
inner flame becomes even brighter.

Day 11

Be totally *available* to the person you are with.

Keywords   **be available**

Day 12

Walk lightly on the earth remaining detached,
not wanting or desiring anything.
How sweet and *simple* is a life without desires.

Day 13

The path is easy for those who have
no preferences.

Keywords   **no preferences**

Day 14

There are no shortcuts to enlightenment
but the company of noble souls ensures that
you experience joy and excitement on the way.
Association determines the direction and goal
of your life.

associate wisely   **Keywords**

Day 15

The only real truth emerges from the *soul*.

Day 16

Remind yourself that *truth* is within you.

truth

Day 17

Never forget that many great souls have fallen
prey to the temptations of this world.
Be aware of the influence of corruption.

be aware

Day 18

Can anyone serve two masters?
Those who *live in the light* can never be
commanded by darkness.

Day 19

In all places, under all circumstances,
remember the presence of *the Eternal*.

remember the Eternal

Day 20

Become so free that your inner joy is not disturbed by any action or reaction from another.

be free

Day 21

A traveller is always at peace when
his burdens are few.
Remember you are
only passing through this life.

Keywords   **only passing through**

Day 22

To give a little is to get a little.
To *give your all* is to grant yourself the greatest
of all gifts.

Day 23

To know the Eternal
requires your *total attention*.

Day 24

Resting within, take a break from the world.

This sequence is an ancient salutation to the sun, traditionally performed at sunrise. This powerful synthesis of movement, breath, visualisation and affirmation captures the quality of self-transformation. Light is now being recognised scientifically as a powerful means to activate the hypothalamus, pituitary and pineal glands. This in turn stimulates the most refined systems in the body - the nervous and endocrine systems. Using the power of the sun and therefore light, this sequence of movements awakens dormant energy at the deepest possible level. A sincere practice of this ancient science, combined with the soulforce Talismans, is the only way to appreciate and understand its potency as a means to *awakening soulforce.*

The best way to perform this sequence is outdoors as early in the morning as possible. To optimise the powerful energy of the sun, just before sunrise and sunset are the best possible times. Otherwise, it is important to do the sequence either before 11 am or after 3pm.

Part Four

The Golden Eagle Sequence

Please remember to imbibe the *key words* at every stage

1. Stand facing the sun with feet together, arms slightly apart from the body, palms forward.

2. Breathe in, folding your fingers into the palms.

3. Breathe out and bend your arms, placing your closed fists onto your chest.

4. Breathing in, raise your elbows out to shoulder level, making sure your fists remain on your chest.

5. Breathe out and open your lower arms, elbows still bent, until the fists face forward.

6. Breathing in, raise fists upwards towards the sky, top of the arms still parallel to the floor.

7. Breathe out and open palms once again. They should be facing inwards towards each other.

8. Breathe in and turn your palms forward to face the sun.

Stand for a few moments breathing in and out slowly, drawing the light from the sun into your palms. Allow the light to flow throughout your whole body.

Affirm: Let there be peace on the earth

9. Breathe in and on the outbreath turn the hands to face inwards.

10. Breathe in and fold your fingers back into the palms.

11. Breathe out and lower fists to shoulder level.

12. Breathe in and draw your fists in towards the chest, elbows still at shoulder level.

13. Breathe out and relax the elbows downwards.

14. Breathe in and lower the hands down to the sides.

15. Breathe out, open your fingers and palms. Allow your body to be completely open, receiving the powerful energy and light from the sun. Be aware that *soulforce* is awakening.

Affirm: Let there be peace on the earth

Reflection

A couple of days after returning to the UK we received a phone call from one of the course participants who was one of the key figures in their work. He said that until we came they had been feeling completely numbed by the traumatic experiences of the war and as a result their faith had completely shut down. Since our visit, however, they felt their belief in their ability to make a difference to their country had been restored. Now they felt they were standing on something solid once again. This is a great starting point for rebuilding your life, for *faith* is the essential element in soulforce awakening and has everything to do with success. The great power we all experienced in those magical moments by the edge of the sea taught me about the true potency of faith.

The impact of my visit to these people upon my own life has been immense, on many different levels. It has shown me beyond any possible doubt that at any given moment a human being's 'pure potentiality' can be ignited. When we are given the right circumstances and the right trigger, something can explode within us. It can be a simple word, gesture, movement or song. When it happens, however, it is like watching a dolphin leaping out of the ocean into the air, catching the first rays of the morning sun on its underside, or a flower opening wide to reveal the most exquisite and unexpected beauty. Life becomes jubilant and vibrantly alive. Working with people whose lives have been shattered by tragedy has opened my eyes to the fact that when people have been broken and destroyed, the simplest knowledge can have the greatest impact upon the human spirit.

Transform boundaries

It is important to remember that the situation I have described in this book didn't happen a long time ago. It is happening *now* and is very real as an ongoing plight. It happened on 17th May 2001 and now *you* are invited to participate in something that connects you to the freedom struggle of a whole nation. This inevitably means that you will become aligned with every human being who is struggling for freedom. If this process can free a nation, what can it do for you as an individual? I invite you to actively participate in this living phenomenon of creating freedom - for yourself as an individual and for the world at large. Isn't it exciting and exhilarating to know that something you do can help to free a nation from the intense struggles of war? Through this practice, you will inevitably transform your own boundaries, your family and circumstances and create immediate healing for yourself and everyone around you. I cannot emphasise this enough. Let me say it again.

As you engage in this practice, you will inevitably transform your own boundaries, your family and circumstances and create immediate healing for yourself and everyone around you.

The most important spiritual principle is that when we engage at any level for a larger cause, something begins to nourish, heal and restore us. This is a *living Talisman*. And please remember that in a war situation, those who suffer the most are the children who represent our future and the future of our planet. Please take a moment to really think about this. Think of the faces of your own children or those of the children around you. What does this mean to you?

We may not be living in a war zone, but we still need to feel a sense of belonging and that our life has purpose and meaning. There is a voice that whispers to us from the depths of our consciousness that tells us we are all trustees of the earth. Gandhi once said,

'The tasks facing us today are enormous, but it is the glory of human nature that there will always be those rare individuals who say, "Let there be danger, let there be difficulties, whatever it costs I want to live to the full height of my being, my feet still on the ground, my head crowned with stars."'

This is such a magnificent statement which captures the great truth that often the greatest power emerges when we face the most impossible situations. With this awareness, the third millennium offers us an amazing opportunity. We all want a world that is healthy and at peace, but the responsibility for creating such a world lies with each one of us. Now that you hold the formula in your own hands, the rest is up to you. Please be aware that this could be the greatest and most transforming moment of your entire life.

About the Author

One of the world's foremost leaders of heart-based spirituality, Mansukh is a man in love with humanity. His every thought, word and deed are designed to help others. He grew up in Kenya's Great Rift Valley within the indigenous tradition of his Gandhian parents. This is where, at a very early age, he learned the secrets of living in harmony with the laws of nature. He has since successfully incorporated his wealth of indigenous knowledge into a scientific career in cancer toxicology. His practical approach to spirituality carries a simple message of compassion, love and deep reverence for the human spirit. In Europe he has become known as 'The Young Gandhi' due to his simple lifestyle and walking tours which bring hope and inspiration to thousands of people. Best selling author of many books and subject of numerous TV documentaries, Mansukh is the presenter of the award-winning TV commentary on the Bhagavad Gita.

The Golden Eagle Sequence can also be found in:

The Secret Power of Light
by Mansukh Patel

Just as Einstein's Theory of Relativity ($E = Mc^2$) revolutionised scientific thought, The Secret Power of Light, as elucidated in this book, promises to redefine your whole way of thinking. A fascinating blend of practical spirituality, scientific fact and a profound understanding of the principles of light that govern our universe.

Body Heart Mind
by Mansukh Patel and Paulette Agnew

Movements for inner strength and wellbeing. This video tape includes a 20 minute daily health programme with preparatory movements, Do-in, spinal activation, sacro-iliac activation, abdominal release and the revolutionary, 'Golden Eagle sequence.'

The words of each Talisman need to be savoured slowly, with deliberation and care. Please understand, these are very powerful truths - *when you live them*.